A Day in the Life of a
Police Officer

by Eric Arnold
Photographs by
Ilene Perlman

SCHOLASTIC INC.
New York Toronto London Auckland Sydney

*Warmest thanks and appreciation to the police officers of
Cambridge, Massachusetts,
for their time and cooperation in helping to create this book.
Special thanks to Officer Kathleen Murphy
for her time, humor, and commitment to the project.
Thanks to Commissioner Perry Anderson, Police Planner Ray Santilli,
Deputy Superintendent Michael Giacoppo, and Officers Edward Burke,
Kenneth Holway, and Edward O'Callaghan.*

*In loving memory of my parents, Esther and Irv.
For Christen and Tali, and for Rochelle, Ben, and Adam.
Thank you, Kate Waters, for your support and humor!
Special thanks to Heidi Kilgras,
and to Jennifer Riggs and Fred Lown.*
— E.A.

*To my parents,
for their love and support*
— I.P.

ISBN 0-590-47443-X

12 11 10 9 8 7 6 5 4 3 2 1   4 5 6 7 8 9/9

Printed in the U.S.A.   08

First Scholastic printing, October 1994

Kathy Murphy is a police officer in Cambridge, Massachusetts. Being a police officer is something she has always wanted to do. "When I was a little girl, my friend's aunt was a police officer, and I thought she had an interesting job. I asked her questions about police work and learned all I could about it.

"I like working with people and helping them, which is what police work is all about."

Kathy works the night shift so she can spend more time with her two young children, Murphy and Mallory. "That way I can be a mom and a police officer! I like taking part in my kids' school activities."

Her other favorite thing to do is play softball. The name of her team is "Third and Charles." She is the pitcher and bats fourth.

When it's time to go to work, Kathy's husband, Mike Aquaro, or her mother, watches the children.

Kathy has to be at the police station for the 4:00 P.M. roll call, so it's time to hurry!

At the station, she has a locker for her clothes, briefcase, and other personal belongings. The locker door is a great place to put up pictures made by Murphy and Mallory.

Before roll call begins, Kathy talks with her partner, Ed Burke, and other officers she knows. "There is a sisterhood and brotherhood of police officers. We try to act as a family and work together. Teamwork is an important part of police work."

At roll call, the lieutenant takes attendance. He informs the officers of police department news and what areas they will be patrolling. Each officer is assigned to patrol a certain area. Kathy rides in a police car, or *cruiser*, in a north Cambridge neighborhood.

A cruiser is built with a *police package* — a powerful engine designed for heavy-duty use and "high performance" at fast speeds. Other important features of a cruiser are:

- an instrument panel equipped with a two-way radio and controls for the emergency lights and siren.
- a light bar on the car roof with blue and red *strobe*, or flickering, lights.
- alley lights on both ends of the light bar, which light up a crime scene or street address.
- strobe headlights and backlights.
- a medical first aid kit in the trunk.

There are two types of siren sounds — a "yelp" and a "wail." Kathy uses the siren and lights so other drivers make way for the cruiser during an emergency.

Other types of police vehicles are the patrol wagon, used for carrying prisoners, and motorcycles. Some police departments also use bicycles and horses.

Kathy rides in Car 5 with her partner.

Before she begins her *tour of duty*, she inspects her cruiser to see that everything is working properly and puts gas in the car. Car 5 is ready to go!

Many people think police work is only the action they see on the news or television shows: high-speed car chases and fighting violent crime. In fact, much of a police officer's time is spent doing *community policing*.

"By patroling the neighborhood regularly, I become part of the community. I get to know the people who live and work there, and they get to know me. They know that I care and am there to help and protect them."

At different times during her shift, she does a *park and walk*. Kathy parks the cruiser and walks around the neighborhoods in her patrol area. She talks with people and listens to their concerns and any complaints they may have.

Or she just walks over to say hello.

The police are called into a situation for four reasons:

1. A person's life is in danger.
2. A person's property is threatened.
3. The peace and quiet of a community is being disturbed. (Police officers are also called peace officers.)
4. A law is being violated or broken.

When a person needs emergency help from a police officer, he or she dials "911" on the telephone. The phone call is answered by the dispatcher in the *communications center* or *radio room* at police headquarters.

After finding out what and where the problem is, the dispatcher radios the police officer patrolling the area nearest the problem to go to the scene.

Kathy is in constant communication with the radio room by using the two-way car radio or the handheld microphone on her shoulder strap, or *epaulet* (pronounced **ep**-uh-**let**).

"When I receive a call on the radio, I'm not always sure what will be going on when I get to the scene. My heart might start to beat fast. Being a police officer is not a scary job to me, because I rely on my training and common sense to help me. If I'm not sure about a situation, I never go in alone. A police officer is trained to call for backup and makes sure other police officers are there to help."

The radio room uses code words to save time. The letters M/V stand for motor vehicle.

> **RADIO ROOM:** Car 5 — Meet the fire department on a complaint of M/V leaking gas on 112 Green Street.
>
> **KATHY:** Received. En route. (We're on our way.)

The police department is often called in on fire emergencies to direct traffic or control the crowds of people who may be watching. Fire trucks need room to work and run their hoses.

There is a possibility of an explosion or fire when a gas leak occurs. Kathy directs traffic on Green Street while the firefighters investigate. Once the leak is brought under control, a tow truck is called in to remove the disabled car, and the street is opened up for regular traffic.

When a person starts a fire on purpose to destroy property, it is called *arson*. The police are called in to help with the arson investigation to find out how the fire started and who set it.

At a recent house fire believed to be caused by arson, Kathy is shown some evidence by an arson investigator from the fire department.

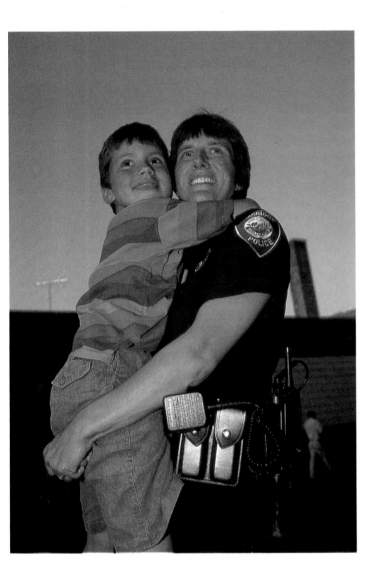

Sometimes Kathy runs into her family while she is on patrol. Her son was shopping nearby with his dad. When Murphy saw his mom, he couldn't resist running over to say "hi" and get a big hug.

No matter where Kathy is patrolling, someone always asks her for directions. "I grew up in Cambridge, which has its advantages. I know all the streets and all the shortcuts!"

When you need directions, asking a police officer is a good idea.

Kathy's uniform identifies her as a Cambridge police officer. The badge and shoulder patch show the seal of the city of Cambridge. Every town or city has its own design for a seal and badge. She also wears a nameplate, and her badge number on her hat and collar.

"It's important for police officers to look professional by being well-groomed and wearing polished black shoes. When I wear a long-sleeved shirt or a jacket, I am required to wear a tie."

Her uniform is designed to provide her with what she will need while on duty. She wears a gun belt with: a holster and gun, two clips of ammunition, handcuffs, and a short stick, called a *baton*. Her pants pocket holds a book of traffic tickets and a pen. Kathy keeps her high-powered flashlight within arm's reach in the cruiser.

The police department issues each officer a uniform when he or she joins the force. The department also gives a set amount of money to an officer to replace a torn uniform or damaged equipment. Kathy goes to the uniform store to shop for items she needs for when she is on duty.

"Police officers are given a gun, which is used only to protect themselves and the people they serve. As a crime is taking place, an officer doesn't just pull her gun out. The only time she draws her gun is if her life is being threatened, someone else's life is being threatened, or if she is in a situation where a person is using a weapon."

Twice a year, Kathy is required to report to a shooting range to practice her skills in the use of a firearm.

A driver fails to stop for a red light. Kathy directs the driver to pull over to the side of the road. She asks to see his driver's license and talks to him about the violation. She fills out a ticket, or *citation* (pronounced sy-**tay**-shun), to give to the driver, and he will have to pay a fine.

Enforcement of traffic laws is an important part of a police officer's job. Car accidents can happen when traffic laws are broken, such as not stopping for a red light or stop sign, or speeding. Police officers are called to the scene when a traffic accident has happened.

Kathy takes an Investigative Report from her briefcase. "There are a lot of reports to be filled out in police work. It's important to write clearly and use proper spelling. This report becomes the official record of the crime and is filed at headquarters."

The person who reported the theft tells Kathy that her new bicycle was stolen from the side of her house. Kathy asks questions to get information she needs to help solve the crime:

- What is a description of the bike?
- What is the serial number of the bike?
- Are there any witnesses who saw the theft?

Kathy informs a neighbor that there have been several bikes stolen in the neighborhood during the last few days.

As Kathy patrols the neighborhood, she keeps an eye out for any suspicious activity. If she sees anyone stealing a bike or riding a bike that was reported stolen, she will make an arrest.

"It's not fun arresting people when they commit a crime, but it's something that has to be done. In some cases, it's very good to get a bad person off the street and into jail — especially if the person has really hurt somebody! Hopefully a person learns a lesson after being arrested and will never break a law again."

"And it's not fun for anyone to spend time in jail."

Sometimes Kathy has to go to the courthouse.

If a person she arrested goes to trial, Kathy may have to be a witness. She will have to tell the judge what she saw and heard when she made the arrest.

It's been a busy shift for Kathy, and it's already dark outside. She is getting hungry — time for a Code 7, which is a dinner break!

All the patrol cars on duty in Cambridge cannot go to dinner at the same time. If they did, no cars would be available to answer calls. The radio room keeps track of where all the patrol cars are. Kathy calls the radio room to see if it is a good time for her to go on a dinner break.

But if there is an emergency while Kathy is on a Code 7, dinner will have to wait!

KATHY:	Car 5 to Control — Is time available for a Code 7?
RADIO ROOM:	Time available. Go ahead. Give us your location where you will be eating.

For dinner, Kathy has one of her favorite foods — pizza with black olives on top! Afterwards, Armando, the owner of the restaurant, fills her in on what's been going on in the neighborhood.

RADIO
ROOM: Car 5 — Go to
70 Cedar Street
to investigate
complaint of a
rabid raccoon in
the yard.

KATHY: Received. 70 Cedar.
En route.

A resident spotted a sickly-looking raccoon near her garbage cans and phoned the police. Due to a recent rabies problem in the area, cruisers have been issued snare poles for trapping rabid raccoons, possums, and other animals.

A rabid raccoon is dangerous because its bite can be very harmful to a person and to a dog or cat. The city has posted signs around the neighborhood to let people know about the rabies problem.

Kathy looks around the area, but doesn't find the raccoon. She tells the resident to call the police again if the raccoon reappears.

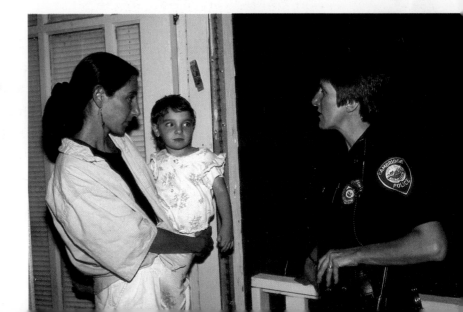

At the city square, street musicians, puppeteers, singers, and other artists perform outside. A crowd gathers to watch a juggler perform. Kathy joins the crowd and enjoys watching people having a fun and safe time.

"The positive benefits I get from being a police officer far outweigh any risks. There is the chance of danger in police work, so I never let my guard down for a moment. Each call is taken seriously.

"One of the best things about being a police officer is when you know you've helped somebody, whether it's a person who is locked out of his car or house, finding a lost child, or solving a crime — there's a good feeling in that."